Seventy Poems

Obediah Michael Smith

Cover image: ©istockphoto.com/Yong Hian Lim
Graphic design: Julia P Ames

ISBN 978-0-557-06089-4

For

Fred D'Aguiar

Keith Russell

Marion Bethel

and

Nicolette Bethel

Dedicated also to writers and scholars who attended the 26th West Indian Literature Conference, March 8th through 10th 2007, at The College of The Bahamas, on New Providence, in The Bahamas, during which time most of the poems in part 1 of this book, Plastic Kool-Aid Cups, were written.

don't worry, spiders,
I keep house
casually.

Kobayashi Issa (1763-1827)

contents

Plastic Kool-Aid Cups

Pack of Dogs Pack of Cards

Plastic Kool-Aid Cups

1

Presents of Mind

for Octavio Paz

how wonderful now is
I must accept, must come to realize
rather than without end,
waiting for what I imagine
is perfection
imagine would be bliss
be it having a million bucks
or having intercourse
with someone desirable
or being in Russia, in Africa
or New Zealand

now though is what I have
is my gift from above
whatever it is full of or short of

why must I live anticipating always
regretting or longing or missing
what was or who was
when now is so full, even if with pain
even if with emptiness
my fist, whenever I wish,
I can fill with my pen
with a poem

2

Gold Fish

for Andrei Tarkovsky

I oftentimes eat films,
other works of art, like a pig

without time to savor them
without time to sip upon them
like wine

without time to dine upon them
as I should, as art deserves
so many times to chew
before I swallow

3

Scent of Green Papaya

for Tran Nu Yen Khe

green frog on green leaf
wet frog on wet leaf
it's raining in Vietnam

4 Allowed To Run About

so many lunatics loose
who should be tied
or in straitjackets, or tried

5 Beheading Dragons

all these monsters
to conquer, to kill,
their heads to cut off
though they keep springing back,
breathing fire

frightening to confront
in life or in sleep

6

Mosquitoes Bees

I'd kill you
if you come too close
with your sting or stick
with whatever weapon,
intending me harm

I'd kill you if you come too close
to harm me, to harming me

7 Virgin Days

life is so fragile
drop it you break it
break it you bought it

8

Recording History

there is as long ago
as there is to go

as much time gone by
as there is to come

what if when the record of time plays,
it merely plays again
like an LP, like a CD
without the merest hiccup
throughout eternity

9

Unable To Go Anywhere

she has some very strong qualities
coupled with some very weak ones

10 Love Birds Love Songs

my poems, however much
they inspire laughter
are usually written
upon death's door,
upon my tomb's floor

when death is near enough
I'd ask her to dance
we would,
with her head at rest
upon my chest
we two circling as the CD,
as the LP goes round

11 Signs Our Times

writing's the anatomy I occupy
ink runs through my veins
and stains and sullies
white page after white page
with poetry

some are, somehow, able to decipher,
able to appreciate

12 Plastic Kool-Aid Cups

there was no listening
to say my poems to,
to put them in - unprepared
to have them fall upon
deaf ears or upon
the night club's red, tiled floor

13

Where Birds Feed

I want poetry on the ground
for anybody, for everybody to pick up

I work along the road, along the street
write poems on my feet

14 Climate for Art

why is the artist made of material
which, when picked up,
when handled, crumbles

unlike a banker, hotelier,
policeman or preacher

15 Engender Art

outside of community usually
now I find myself
outside of community
of artists also

this pains me in ways
too difficult to bear
this I never expected

16 Look Seek

someone who could overlook
what I need overlooked
who could see me and would have me
I seek such a one

17

Press for Time

for Jennifer

my poems result from
paper I pick up or walk on

what's left upon them,
remains upon them to be read,
are my footprints
or my fingerprints

what can I do about my features
about the configuration
of my Deoxyribonucleic acid

about the stains I make,
the marks I leave

18 Scrap Match

why are these persons in your pipe,
burning, stinking up the place,
stinking up the room I'm in,
torturing me while they are
elsewhere, free,
Fyodor Dostoevsky, Pintard, K.B.

19 Up Against Them

against these persons
whom you mention
with such antipathy
or up against them,
they up against you
like lovers in bed
as bare as infants
only just born
cuddling, soft
rolling round

20 Billy Goat Gone

I am arguing
with your cigarettes
their smell in your pores

with your alcohol
in your arteries and veins,
in your brain

arguing with confusion, with pain

wasting pearls
I fling like jacks, like dice

with what, with whom I gamble
not entirely clear

whatever I throw though,
whatever I loose
I lose

21 Mail Boat Gone

she smells like
a crocus sack
full of plums

22 Incense Ever Since

for M.B.

how close she is to me still,
she is to me now
smell sweet, in eyes, ears, nostrils
here wrapped in her black, wool shawl
in this lecture hall

23

Munch Light

there is an orchestra
of listening ears
while Patti Glinton
chews chunks of
Shift In The Light
for us to swallow
to digest easily

24 Blistex

herpes simplex
complicates my life
simplifies my life
restricts involvement
socially and otherwise

must interact otherwise
my eyes in books
those I read as well as those
with blank, lined pages
to write across

books as if to hide my face in
for shame, from staring eyes
from pity or scorn

even the touch of admiration
or affection, unbearable

with voice or eyes
I hide between lines of verse
among words
until the plague passes

it passes only to come again
thus this affair on sheets of paper,
with alphabet

25

Point of Laughter

with poem stab, with pen stab
repeated jabs of verse
for who assembles to listen
victims of verbs and adverbs
of adjectives, half-rhymes,
near rhymes

with these, do it to them
until they're on the floor in stitches
holding their sides
laughing at tragedy averted, avoided
at what could have been bloody

26

By and By
for MacDonald-Smythe

too high above me
for words to break
between us like waves

though words like bullets fly
hit some, miss some

I have my lips to nurse
sick to tend, shame to hide
like shirt tail
mom would demand
gently but firmly
I put in my pants
tuck in rather than
shirt tail waving like flag
like sails in wind

one woman I loved
but she's dead now
lost her long before that though
two-year affair, lasted until Sonia,
my sister was born

loved this woman crazily
for several hours
hot like water for tea,
warm the next day, cool the next

wide-eyed about her still
when I see her

greedily I take her in

looking like licking
like cats, like kittens

27 Oceans Seas Cays

cob of the West Indies
as if growing in Trinidad, Guyana or Bar-
bados

islands of The Bahamas
like a few corn grains adhering to it

some imagine us adhering to it
not at all, not represented

upon what level most a part, most apart
politics, culture, athletics, geography

what are they, what are we
where are they, where are we
where and in what things do we meet

28 Blacksmiths and Carpenters

nails I had driven in with my verse
were difficult to extricate
with other verses, by other readers

they had to drive theirs in as well
with whatever hammer in their hand

anvil to pound upon, to echo noise

29

Empty Bowls

for N.T-B.

she commits adultery
on the mike on Wednesday nights

audience assembled resemble Oliver
wanting more porridge

30 **Love Lies Bleeding**

busy expressing her love
in her way
I, busy, expecting it expressed
in some other way

too busy, disappointed, regretting
to notice all her effort
all the love out poured
from her oftentimes

onto the floor and overlooked
not noticed by this busy,
disappointed man

expecting some other hand
another woman

31

Coconut Bark

for Marsha Pearce

sepulcher for supper,
clean place to lie
sheets to lie in, to die in

borrowed tomb to rest a while
resurrection comin'
early Sunday morning

no need to weep
for who's a stone's throw away

throw me away all you wish
I won't go away

once in the universe
unable to get rid of who,
even if dead, even if killed,
even if dragged, leaves blood tracks
or mud tracks

especially a murder
committed in snow

snow to cross to warmer weather
coconut jelly, coconut water

belly full of goodness,
too full to complain
to need anything but ballet,
a bowl full of grapes
a bed full of breasts
and thighs and nipples

Aware of Wolves

32

Stravinsky-tranquility
what distilled waters
at the core of this man's music
however troubled his edges are
are his metaphors of war
wars to pass through, water to cross

fire-water, coupled with dreams
he's velvet as well as sandpaper

water without edge
unless you fall in it, fall on it
unless your boat capsizes
and what's in it cuts you up
unless it cuts your breath,
your belly open, you in half

water you swallow, smooth as could be
as could be expected

art lets us get off at the next stop
"Bus stop!"
old lady in the back seat
arrives where she's going

I get off at a point of knowing
abruptly ends the poem

art must not show off
must show its face, its ass
and be gone, and be off

stage to vacate, to leave
like another clean page

33 House of Flies

big, stinkin' flies
fill up my place
as if something were rotten
as if I were in Denmark

with swatter like sword
I slash and slash
as angry as Hamlet
until they're all dead
until they are dead
and the play ends
and the day ends

their last day, my new day
my good news day

34

Petals Wings

for M.B.

certain emotional equipment
lacking, to fill in the gap, to bridge it

Bridget and me, our affair in trouble,
unable to fix it

advised by friends of hers,
friends of mine
to fall away, to follow her fear,
voice of it, to the next station

take the train to the nation's other city
didn't think she'd have gone far away,
foolish me

did not begin ringing my bell
sufficiently soon, to call her back

our bed full of sweets
already she was on the street
places to go, things to achieve
I among the sheets, cocooned in these
my butterfly to fly later
join up with her, catch up with her
among petals of wild, field flowers

we each have two daughters
with other partners

35

Defeated Rise

fever blisters have,
for so very long
been barriers between
me and my desire
for someplace in society
pretty someone

impressive to appear
in public with, lips ornamented
with fever blisters, with cold sores

humiliated, humbled
perfect place for poetry
for poems to spring from

will my spring ever come

36

Fix Me Soup

for L.M.

cuckoo soup on Sunday,
way I like to be/when I like to be
fixed

37 Partnership

though she does not read
or seldom does
she provides a lot to read
to write about

I sing out in response to her
inserted in my life
as sharply as a knife

shape of her hips in time
as well as in the seat I provide

could such a woman
have been made from
the rib from my side

into the side of Christ
Roman soldier drives a spear
water from the side of Christ
wash my vision clear, my slate clean

notes of so many sins written on it,
honest

38 Professor

for MacDonald-Smythe

drink
a tall glass
of her
every time
I see her
glasses full
of her
laughter

39 Hailstones

hey God, hello, where's my halo
you promise I could have one

halos like Frisbees, tossed about
for quick, small dogs to leap up to catch

40

Love Vine

for M.B.

like straps
arms about the back
about the neck
over the shoulders
beneath arms in an embrace
some women I meet and love
I want to buckle my arms about
I want to be strapped together with
for weeks, for days

some of them
I've held without clothes
with no clothes between us
to separate us

41 Sausages

what pieces of us
to share with them
like sliced bread

we'd keep the butt ends, the day end
to put sausage on
to push sausage between

42 Atlantic Wide

art intervenes in life
makes connections where gaps exist
which otherwise would continue to
as well as continue to widen,
to lengthen, as if upon water,
upon waves, drifting open like wounds,
like legs, for uninvited,
unapproved of intercourse

43 Boughs of Holly

holy hoe,
hoeing to plant hollies
to have when Christmas
rolls around, comes along
to collect
must have enough to offer
to satisfy

44

Where Stations Converge

for A. Sears & A. Gray

MPs in Rawson Square
in suits, with their satchels
calling for or waiting impatiently
for chauffeurs

bust of Milo Butler,
made of bronze, in the square also
Victoria on her throne, in marble,
in gown, with scepter in hand

square like toy, its two halves
come together, come apart
where Bay Street is, where traffic runs

on a bus going home
I see MPs, so very well
so very wealthy, so well dressed
I admire as well as envy
the state they're in, in Rawson Square
with Milo Butler, with Victoria,
regal, royal

status of all this, of all these
touching to me, touch even me
lowly as I am, little as I am,
humble as I am

ability of some of us,
from humble beginnings, to rise up,
able, like cream,
to rise to the top

some among us, beneath us
somehow, forever stuck in shit,
catching shit, taking shit, doing shit

I in this flux, in this dynamic
wondering about it
wondering why it is

what vehicle some of us gat
some of us on, some of us catch
which others can't

cannot or don't want
can or cannot get on
like that wave a surfer
must await to get on
without which, on his belly,
he'd have to wade to shore

some of us wading in,
others bathing in blood
caught in bullets flying, firing
instead of rain, instead of
blessings, falling vertically
upon us all

45

Familiar Mine

for N. Burnett

why are you tickling me
with attention I could hardly bear
snuggling up to me
under my arms, snickering, giggling

how could I help but crack up
break up

disarmed by your entering, intervening
without needing permission,
without asking

delicious, presumptuous

46 Caribbean Queen

her slippers slapping the road
as she crosses,
clapping appreciation

driver gracious enough to stop
to stop traffic
for her journey to grow on
to make her feel like Walter Raleigh
made the queen feel
when he spread his coat in mud
for her to enter her carriage

47

Belt to Unbuckle

could her pussy, any pussy
make my ends meet
make me touch me
sweets like lollypop
in a child's cheeks

48

City Lights or Lights Out

bringing children into the world
for someone or other to take out
I, unable to find anyone to go out with

49

Fire Draws Figures

for Desiree Cox

image drawn by fire
who is it burning up
who was it thrown in the flames
was it Shadrach, is it his sister
is it the woman in him
revealed by fire,
its transforming power

caught in flames, unable to escape
must pay to exit, to exist
insufficient in my bank account
to bribe the devil to set me free
to release my family
antithetical to the colors of the rainbow
to the colors sun and rain clouds make
the colors flame makes
witch on fire, roasting

50

Egg & Spoon

so much work
to align ourselves
with one someone
to remain aligned
like two in a sack, in a sack race
day and night,
night and day
until something breaks

51 On Earth Circus

earth is a bicycle
I, at times, even oftentimes
forget how to ride

at times for hours
at times for days
weeks sometimes
I am unable to get my balance

52 Word Mechanics

I leak poems like a car leaks oil
or like a car, its radiator leaking

Pack of Dogs Pack of Cards

53 Bite off To Chew

a gun
like its much larger relative, war
is a toy
that has gotten out of hand

Shovel In Sand

54

not all of his poems
can you dig with either
not all of his poems
are a hammer in your hand

55

Time I Wed

reluctant to lie down with myself
like two men in bed

I want a woman to come between us
to get between us
come push us apart

56 Disguise With Smile

without a clue
without caring to have a clue
she'd smile the sweetest smile
just as her dad used to

I'd wonder what they know
or knew that I didn't
wonder if they got it
or caught it

could they have missed the boat,
the bus and wear such a bright smile
such a big smile, sweet smile
without missing a screw

57 Are Days Numbered

ticking off days
days ticking away

ticking of days
like ticking bombs set
set to go off

top of our days
set to blow off in time

we keep our black dresses
our black outfits
to gather about
a hole in the ground

58 Aborted Missions

many in our community
with guns, pulling triggers,
should have been ejaculated
into condoms and disposed of

the gallows, Privy Council,
other complications,
would need not ever have arisen

these persons,
allowed into existence,
into being,
without appreciation for sunrise,
falling stars,
without appreciation
for squawking seagulls
hovering over our harbors

59 Henri Matisse

what he manages to cut out, to leave out
what he leaves in, somehow, breathing still

he never cuts the lungs apart, across
he never cuts the heart out

60 Ire

who was a friend of mine
is a dough-white bore,
time I turned upon her as Picasso would
upon the women in his life
after he'd gotten enough pictures
out of them, when they were as empty
as tooth paste tubes
she was empty to begin with

61 Glass Huts

not only elephants have hides,
we too have our hiding places,
within thick skins

from slings and arrows,
from sticks and stones,
from words hurled at us to hurt us

62

Sandy Beaches

swept up like skirts,
out of a sort of sleep,

alive in ways I had not been
since mystery severed ties
I had with pelicans, years ago

love disaster, that disaster,
she was born ten years after

able somehow to stir me so,
head to toe

long long spoons, in lemonade, in ice tea

we're having lunch this afternoon
umbrella above our heads
tourists about us, scantily clad,
imagine they're in paradise

we know we are

63 Russian Paint

Kandinsky, convince me
to buy your art
to sell my own

64

A Han Ta Sleep In

I getting so wear out
I almos like a page yur could tear out
so tired, eyes tired

at dis computer all night long
feel like all life long

life still long or short now
like a pencil yur write wid
and broke an sharpen
and broke an sharpen
tell it only a nub, a stub in yur fis
yur hardly could hole

I hardly could hole up
I better lie down
I better go sleep, slip inta dream lan

65 In Two Nights

i
wanted to be
the wick in her wax
to whisper in her ear

ii
out of her mouth
almost slipped a poem
I wanted as much
as I wanted her tongue

iii
I wanted to make your little phone ring
I wanted to light up your numbers

iv
cruel to make stale jokes
about cold Canadian buns,
about bums in winter,
freezing beside the road

with buns bare in bed,
up against each other,
we try to keep warm,
away from the Tropics

66

One Stormy Night

far from home, far from perfect
on this night, in this land

in a boat, I entered history
the roughest waves lashing it

haunted still by the waves' roughness
by that night's blackness

67 String

pop this, these words
I've strung together
just for you to wear

necklace, bracelet, made of beads
all over the museum floor
all over the dance floor, bouncing

upon hands and knees
as if playing jacks
quickly trying to pick them up

beads I now replace with words
string through these, who can see
who can pop before time ends

68 Kites And Dresses

language, unlike a spool of thread
has no beginning and no end

69

Water Clear As Glass

it is all theft, isn't it
living and writing
transferring, translating
one thing, something
into something else

transferring something
from one place to someplace else

usually from somewhere without
to somewhere within

it's all theft, isn't it
the evening sun upon the sea
my trying to capture it
to snatch this evening
from August

70 Pack of Dogs Pack of Cards

dog getting his ass chewed up,
chewed off
by whoever in the pack
is biggest, is baddest

the most angry on the street
greeting the most passive

chewed up and yelping,
helpless, howling until allowed
to get up and run

I run to the door,
too late to see,
what is for who lives over-the-hill,
in inner city, Nassau

as thrilling as a bull fight
in the middle of Madrid,
is for who's Spanish

www.ingramcontent.com/pod-product-compliance
Ingram Content Group UK Ltd.
Pitfield, Milton Keynes, MK11 3LW, UK
UKHW020237250726
13967UKWH00001B/415